Gather Up Your Soul

GATHER UP YOUR SOUL

Photography copyright © 2013 by Sarah M. Clarehart (except where noted)

1st Edition, published by Highpoint Life.
For information write to info@gatherupyoursoul.com

First Edition
ISBN: 978-0-9891054-0-8

Library of Congress Control Number: 2013934882

ISBN: 978-0-9891054-0-8 (hardbound)

Cover and Interior design by Sarah Clarehart

10 9 8 7 6 5 4 3 2 1

Gather Up Your Soul

Poems by Bartholomew John Erbach

HIGHPOINT

ACKNOWLEDGMENTS

I'd like to express my gratitude to a few special people who played a key role in making this book a reality. I am deeply thankful to the late, great John Golden who first showed me the path to myself and poetry; to Jim Dinneen S.J. for receiving my spirit and my early poems with joy and reverence; to my CFT classmates who made writing poetry feel like hitting a walk-off home run, and especially to Katie Malachuk whose coaching and friendship nurtured this book into existence. And finally, gratitude beyond words to my sister Sarah Clarehart (aka Daryl) who brought it all to life with grace and beauty.

For My Main Muse

Margaret Mary

Whose Love Is the Source
Of All That Is Good
In My Life

The Fog

The fog surrounds my heart
Follows me
From coast to coast
Rolls in and stays

So misty and light
So thick at night
Its horn bellows
Mourning softly

I raise my cup
Begging
For succor and peace
For a clearing to see

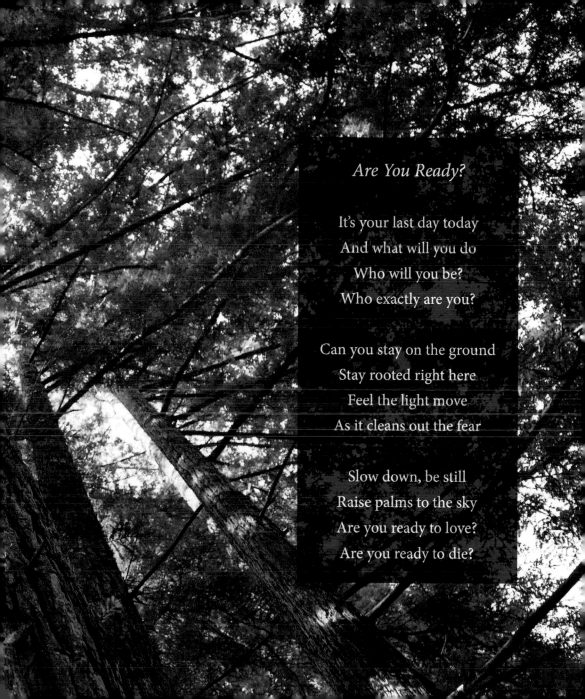

Are You Ready?

It's your last day today
And what will you do
Who will you be?
Who exactly are you?

Can you stay on the ground
Stay rooted right here
Feel the light move
As it cleans out the fear

Slow down, be still
Raise palms to the sky
Are you ready to love?
Are you ready to die?

Piercing the Trance

My son, Tim, dashed into the street one night
She slammed her brakes

But her SUV sent his 16-year-old body
Sailing through the air

This pierced my trance
My coming and going
Hurrying and worrying
Getting there...where?

The lights flashed all around him
As EMTs fastened his body and head to a gurney
He bravely tried to comfort us
But the trance was pierced

There was only now, now
Only fervent prayers to
A God so real
I could see him kneeling
Near Tim's side

These moments
Stop the stories
We keep alive
And shake us
As out of a dream

They pierce the trance
Pierce our hearts
Till love flows freely
Till life knows only now

What Wants to Be Seen?

What is it   We're nervous

In us   And shaky

That wants   Jealous

To be seen?   And frayed

So fragile   But stirring

And scared   Within us

So hungry   Our heart

And lean   Makes a stand

When light   See me!

Comes our way   It exclaims

We run   A plea

To the shade   Or demand?

Beauty in the Shadows

Is there beauty in the shadows?
Is there music in the weeds?
Are there linings to the darkness?
Does blindness help you see?

What masks the light
That shines all day?
The force that pulls from under
Till slowly we
Start breaking free
Through small steps
Of surrender

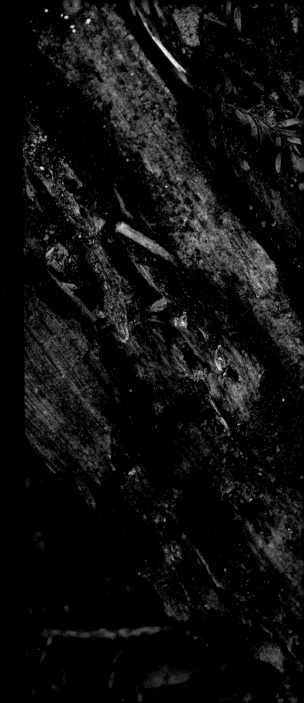

Embrace the Fear

Cold animal fear
Ferries me back
Thumping heart
Down on my knees
To humility's shore

I behold this frothing fear
It lives and breathes
Its painful wisdom
No more running
Nor hiding
Just exhale surrender

Now I know
Embrace the fear
Hold its hand
Shed another layer
And feel fresh air tingle
The newest growth
Of tender skin

Unshakable Faith

The winds bring the fear
To my doorstep again
I struggle to hear
A simple amen

I can't seem to find
My love for myself
I can't seem to feel
That spiritual health

Unshakable faith
That's what I want
No quaking at night
Please call off the hunt

Unshakable faith
Where are you now?
I'm ready to sign up
I'm ready and how

The Dawn Does Come

The dawn does come
Even to the darkest nights
Close your eyes
And all is lost
You are alone
You fail to see
The spirit whose hand
Awaits your touch

Open your eyes
Slowly take it in
The leaves, the light
The pink-blue sky
Its stillness speaks
To your troubled heart
Do not fear
I am still with you
I never left

The dawn does come
Even to the darkest nights

A (Sacred) Pause

I rest my head in your embrace
A moment in a holy place
A pause to feel a sense of calm
To still the fear, a soothing balm

Fourth Week, First Contemplation

The aroma of bread
Fills the room
But not the emptiness

Alone with her pain
She tries to return to
Daily life without her son

She aches, until he appears
Resplendent, alive

He draws her to himself
Embracing her without words
Softly he kisses her forehead

For one tender moment
It is the deepest consolation

Be Gentle with Yourself

Be gentle with yourself
You did not invite
The storms that
Rolled down the mountain
Cold and withering
You sustained them though
And kept walking along the path
Let go the lashing memories
Warm your hands
With your light
Your heart wants to dance
Strike up the band

Ode to Walt

Eyelids closed, head back
I see but orange sunburst lines
Etched somewhere
Connecting the warmth of the sun
To my flush cheeks

A long staccato string of song
From that bird beyond
Flies forth as
Clouds amble by
I hear your hymn across
A century and more
Your full-throated praise
Of the universe

That sensual and soft
Ode to nature's rhyme
The divine
In our daily walk

I Hear Your Voice

Magnolias scream
A cardinal's song
The cherries weep
As days grow long

I hear your voice
Still, sweet and soft
This subtle light
Lifts grace aloft

Dusk settles in
My heart is king
No room for fear
First day of Spring

The Cricket

Cicadas clamor with desire
They pulse a steady beat
A rousing summer symphony
Crescendos with the heat

What's that? The lonely cricket's sound
Its quiet heart does send
A solitary sentry stands
To signal summer's end

Equinox

So many false starts fill the air
Or do my true starts falter?
They seem to lose their steam in time
Their power to cross over

Now Autumn marks a shift of sorts
A turning of the leaves
As trees surrender fingertips
That touch down through the breeze

I wonder what's in store for me
What do the stars have planned
What winds will whip into my life
When will I raise my hand

To say, okay, I need to pray
I need to settle down
Like stirring leaves that finally stop
As green reverts to brown

A Snow Covenant

Healing snowflakes fall
From heaven's heart
To all
Who with open mouth
Catch them on their tongue
Like children
Who can't recall
Their fall, at all

This is Creation

This is Creation
Today is the beginning
Again
Outside my window
The rising sun
Illuminates a seagull
The warm glow cradles her
As she gently glides
Above the house tops
All the birds are singing now
They do not remember yesterday
Or fear tomorrow
This is Creation
Today is the beginning
Again

What Time Is It Please?

for Eckhart Tolle

I was lost in the woods
So fearful and sad
My memories hunting
My nights scary bad

I spotted a hawk
Soaring high on the breeze
I asked him this question
"What time is it please?"

He looked at me puzzled
And with truth did avow
The answer is simple
"Of course it is now!"

The eagle chimed in
And so did the bear
Wond'ring why would I ask…
Saying "What else is there?"

The Glory of Now

The glory of sleep
John playing a tune
Dinner with friends
And light from the moon

My dog on the couch
Getting new biz
Stuck at a light
Tim's Chemistry quiz

Rain on the roof
Figuring how
A train rolling by
The glory of now

Fishers of Men

Fishing lines to water drop
The clouds roll by
Hawks float on top

Tim says, Dad, let's move the boat
John pulls anchor
We slowly float

A time for boys
And father who
Is trying hard
Could harder still

Become the man
They'll emulate
Respect and follow
Not too late

To learn to love
And to believe
That life is lived
On days like these

Dark to Light

Light to dark

Dark to light

Shadows fall

Disturb the night

My will is strong

It wants control

It thinks it's right

It wants my soul

Past to future

Future past

My peace of mind

Just doesn't last

And so I wrestle

Oh, please let go

Please help me feel

The love you know

Ballast of Silence

I drift ahead
Waves and wind
Rocking me
No wheel to steer

Like swirls through space
My life evolves
Like energy dancing
Through time and gravity
Like flickers of flame
In the dark

Still, I feel steady
My ballast of silence
Signals the story's end
And flings open
The longing of my heart

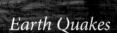

Earth Quakes

Earth quakes	A hundred billion stars evolved
Earth shakes	Galactic gas and dust
It happens all the time	Just one of hundred billions more
But when your walls	Beyond our earthen crust
Start swaying it	
Sends shivers down your spine	Small shifts awaken
	In our hearts
We're living on a floating orb	The presence of a force
That circles 'round a star	They pierce the trance
Which also circles	And let light in
In its way	To take another course
Through milky stretches far	

Timeless Tears

On an impossibly glorious day
Serenity floats
Beneath the hawk way on high
Bluest sky, greenest hills
Life used to be clouds,
With a side of sun
Now it tastes sublime

Cascades of white vapor
Dance with ballet grace
Two clouds drift gently
Into each other's arms
With the softest,
Slowest kiss

Sun rays swirl a milky edge
Radiating reds and pink
A fibrous matrix
That stretches its wispy fingertips
The conductor of all creation

And then the portal opens—
Transforming all
Now undulating gentle waves like syrup
Shimmer to a Presence
With land and sky and sun
Slipping into my soul
And I am caught again in rapture
Stunned with timeless tears

We Wait to Love

You wait
To love
Yourself
Too busy now

There are bills
And projects
And worries
And things…

There's tomorrow
To consider
And, oh, that
Pesky past

But love
Wants out
Into the world
Right now

You wait
for what?
Your busy seconds tick
And tick, and tock
A fearful clock
And so
You wait

For what?

Whitewater Wisdom

The captain calls out
Hard left, then hard right
We're rocking down rapids
Whitewater delight

The river runs high
The current so swift
A hurricane filled
These banks with a gift

Your balance gets tested
By pillows and trees
And swirls that turn rafts
With such dizzying speeds

The guide shouts beware
Of freezing your gaze
On an upcoming rock
Or an obstacle maze

By focusing there
You will not see the way
You will steer into trouble
You will ruin your day

Let go of the fear
And flow where it's free
Just paddle that way
Your composure is key

This wisdom of water
Can carry you far
Like floating through space
Beneath the North Star

They're peaceful by nature
If never provoked
But ruffle their feathers…
The truce is revoked!

Tickling Alligators

They bellow in May
Those al-li-ga-tors
They dance in the moonlight
And hunt near the shores

At 800 pounds
They pack quite a pop
They're old and they're slow
But they're stronger than snot

I wrestled one once
It fought quite the fight
I wouldn't give in
Gave all of my might

With short bursts of speed
They'll clamp down their jaws
And drag you and spin
And thrash without pause

You'll faint as they chomp
You'll soon lose your pulse
You'll know that you've lost
When you start to convulse

They'll kill you and eat you
With one single bite
No mayo or mustard
Just death roll tonight

Then one day a stranger
Said why do you fight?
What pulls you down
In the mud with such might?

An easier way
She said with a smile
Is to just rub its belly
Relax and beguile

I tried this approach
It grew meek as a sheep
I tickled its nose
It soon was asleep

So the moral to this
Is STOP WRESTLING SO MUCH!
Try tickling instead
It's all in the touch!

The Fog Lifts

The fog lifts
Evaporates
Light lances
The sun is back!

An orange rim
Rings the ocean
As donkeys appear
Curious heralds

We laugh again
Waves meet the mountains
John howls
A clearing to see

Now

Now when I behold the moon
Its phasing nights from black to white
Silver sutras of slivered light
I will behold the cycles of my life

Now when I hear a bird
Sing songs of living so assured
I will pay attention
To here and now
Answer the call
That is my vow

Now when I sense the flight
A butterfly within my sight
As it flutters into my cocoon
I will open up
A rose in June

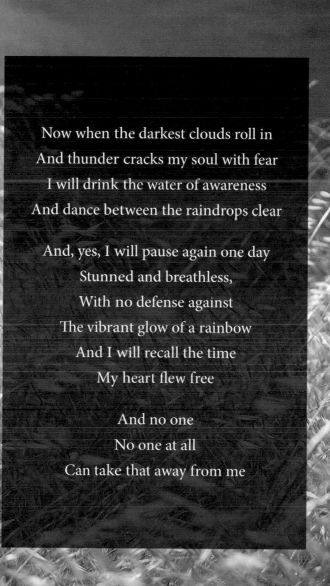

Now when the darkest clouds roll in
And thunder cracks my soul with fear
I will drink the water of awareness
And dance between the raindrops clear

And, yes, I will pause again one day
Stunned and breathless,
With no defense against
The vibrant glow of a rainbow
And I will recall the time
My heart flew free

And no one
No one at all
Can take that away from me

Welcome Home

From the street
I can see the colored lights
Of our Christmas tree
I walk up two sets of stairs
To our porch
High above the street
House all lit up
Ring the doorbell
There's Luna
Tail wagging
Margaret lets me in
Hi honey
Luna so excited
Races like a crazy beagle
Three times around
The dining room table
Doing the Daddy's-gonna-feed-me! dance
While Tim practices Linus and Lucy
On the piano in the parlor
French student John
Hits the second syllable
In "Hello Pa-*pa*"
On the fireplace mantle
Gold lights and candles
Illuminate Father Christmas and his friends
Dinner's cooking
Angels fill the house
I'm home